HOW CAN MOVING MY SHOULDERS UP AND DOWN HELP ME GET MORE OUT OF LIFE?

And other frequently asked questions by beginners in sophrology

Anne Jamelot-Bonnaillie

© 2019 Anne Jamelot-Bonnaillie

Published by: Books on Demand GmbH

12/14 rond-point des Champs-Elysées

78 008 Paris, France

Impression: Books on Demand GmbH

Norderstedt, Allemagne

ISBN: 9 782 322 104 963

Legal deposit: July 2019

To my father, Jean-Pierre.

He would have illustrated this book had I had the time to ask him.

To Bernard Santerre,

Who, from wherever he is up there, inspired me when I felt doubt setting in.

Translation: Jenny Scott

Contents

Preface..7

By means of an introduction...9

What's sophrology?..12

What's the point of paying attention to our sensations?...............14

What happens in a sophrology session?..........................19

What's the point of talking about our experience at the end of a session?..21

    Why use the 'I' form?..21

    What if I don't talk at the end of the session?...........24

What's the point of being 'aware'?...................................27

    Why?...27

    What do we have to do to become aware?................28

    Isn't all this a rather self-centred journey?.................31

    How come being more aware makes us more active?...............32

How long before I get better? When do I see results and start to feel well?...34

    What does 'feeling well' mean?..................................34

Can sophrology cure me from insomnia?........................38

What's the recommended number of weekly sessions?...............41

    Yes, BUT, it isn't the same at home as it is in a session with a sophrologist..41

What's the best time of the day to practise?................................42

Where should I practise?..43

What does it mean: to 'work on ourselves'?......................................45

Why practise standing rather than lying down?................................50

Do we never practise sophrology lying down?................................52

The importance of the discourse..53

What will practising sophrology do for me?....................................55

What's a sensation? What is it we have to feel?..............................60

Yes, but... what do you call 'a sensation'?......................................60

What do you recommend: one-to-one or group sessions?..............66

The notion of confidentiality..67

How can moving my shoulders up and down help me get more out of life?..68

And what if we can't move our shoulders or do any other exercise?...70

What happens next? What is it meant to do for me?......................71

I can't manage to concentrate, how can I improve this?................76

What's the point of living in the present moment?......................77

Doesn't living in the present all the time become rather tiresome?...78

They say sophrology helps develop creativity. How come?...........80

By means of a conclusion..83

Thank you..85

Preface

Anne was writing down the answers to these questions that she had, for years, been asked at her sophrology sessions. These answers had been constantly refined over the years and when I saw what she was doing, I was both interested and excited at the thought of being able to share and to pass on her personal experience, in that very own unique style of hers! It was only too obvious to me how useful and valuable this would be.

Since then, it has been my pleasure to share with Anne her thoughts and sensitivity through to the final stage of this book you are now holding in your hands.

So you are welcome to this interview in which you will find a number of new theories, techniques and clinical case studies as yet unpublished.

What Anne Jamelot has created here is a compilation of questions frequently asked by participants in group or individual sophrology sessions. Established professional sophrologists who are knowledgeable of and experienced in the methods and philosophy of sophrology may be surprised by some of the questions – and answers.

However, even though a question like "what is the point of living in the present moment?" may be surprising, it is nonetheless a question worth answering.

Anne Jamelot chose to write in the same way as she talks to people: she talks straight; her language is accessible and it comes free from technical jargon. She always expresses herself with sensitivity and with frequent humour.

Happy reading!

Soizick Roulinat

By means of an introduction

I began practising group sophrology in January 1995 and it is from this date that my inventory of frequently asked questions begins.

There are many questions that a sophrologist leaves unanswered. Some may be sent back to the person in question with the claim that any understanding and any answers to such questions should come from one's own experiencing; a sophrologist's own experience isn't meant to influence others in their own practice. There are however other questions which are worth spending time over. In fact, I think that if I hadn't answered the latter my students perhaps would not have continued with their practice of sophrology; this would have been a great shame especially when I consider all the progress they have made since.

Passing comment: I don't believe I ever influenced any clients' experience since I've always kept to myself what I personally experience in the sessions I guide. I have even been frequently reproached – in jest of course – for not explaining everything to them; but my response hasn't changed: I would not be doing them a service if my own personal development were to influence theirs for the point of sophrology is to forge one's own opinions, to develop a critical mind and to become independent. I believe that all experiences, even that of passing discomfort, leads to a person investing himself more rather than expecting the professional practitioner to give him all the answers. The technique is simple, that is true, but we need to do a lot of work on ourselves to get to that simplicity and it pays off when we see the deep lasting effects that can actually happen quite quickly.

I've also organised many information sessions and talks to make sophrology more widely known, and this has enabled hundreds of people to start practising this discipline – not necessarily with me – with a good understanding of what to expect, and with fewer preconceived ideas.

It's been a while since I wanted to put down on paper those explanations that I've so naturally given over the years; firstly, so I don't have to talk about them any more (I must admit I am getting tired of it!), secondly for use by other sophrologists, those practising sophrology and anybody wanting to know what the point of sophrology is ; those who think they've understood it all because they've been to one session, those who think it is all about relaxation, or exam and childbirth preparation... Finally, I decided to write this because a large number of students have encouraged me to do so for some time now.

I've referred especially to the first and second level of relaxation techniques because it is really during those sessions that people ask the most basic questions. There are 12 levels altogether but I only teach the first five. The answers I give to these questions tend to determine whether new participants are likely to continue with, or put an end to their practice of sophrology.

As a teacher of physical education, I am well accustomed to large groups of adults and in my teaching methodology I continuously refer to sophrology. In this book, I write as I speak to those who attend my information events or conferences. What I wanted to do was to write a book everyone could understand, so theoretically, you shouldn't need a dictionary here!

Enjoy reading and whoever you are, thanks for taking part in the game!

Anne Jamelot-Bonnaillie

What's sophrology?

Sophrology is a neologism which has its roots in three Greek words:

SÔS: meaning 'harmony'

PHREN: 'mind' or by extension 'consciousness'

LOGOS: 'language, study, discourse'

Sophrology is the study of harmonious consciousness, or the study of consciousness in harmony. This harmony can be likened to some instrumental band or orchestra in which each instrument has its own function and uniqueness, both in terms of physical aspect and sound. Despite this, and also thanks to this, all the instruments in this orchestra have the potential to create harmony. We need to pay attention, be disciplined and we have to work at creating harmony. Sophrology is therefore the study of consciousness in all its aspects, and our observation of how this harmony is created.

Sophrology is a scientific method which includes many techniques (dynamic relaxations, sophronisations) and it is based on phenomenology.

In short, phenomenology is a philosophy which consists in approaching any phenomenon as if it were for the very first time, without prejudice, without judgement, without expectation, commentary, analysis or interpretation. So we approach each aspect of our environment, ourselves or whatever else as if it were for the first time and we do this now or at any point in the future, without prejudice, judgement or analysis, just purely and simply being in the experience, in the perceiving of the moment, and in the feeling.

We just pay attention to our sensations wherever they are in the body, whatever they may be, and no matter the outcome: that is what we do each time we meditate.

In this sense, sophrology is meditation. It is a set of dynamic meditation exercises guided by a sophrologist, laid out in a very structured and clever way by Alfonso Caycedo who was the creator of the method in the 1960s.

What's the point of paying attention to our sensations?

It helps you become more aware.

Not only aware of your sensations but also your thoughts, feelings in the present moment, without prejudice, without judgement. Nothing is positive or negative and there are no commentaries, nor any interpretations or analysis.

Difficult! Imagine you are interested in sensing how you are breathing as if it were the first time; you know very well it isn't the first time you do this, but you have to pretend it is. You put yourself in that same state of mind in every moment of sophrology practice. You welcome the sensations that you notice are happening, you observe how they are at each point and without any preconceived ideas or expectations. Just listening in, being in the moment. So you need to set aside all you already know about your breathing, everything you have already experienced about it so you can be right there, at the point of listening, in the present moment, without any expectations.

Even though you know what happens to you when you breathe and you know what the point of breathing is, you put all this to one side; you suspend all judgement and you make the most of the opportunity to be receptive to who you are right here and right now.

Preconceived ideas and judgements are like blinkers: they prevent us from discovering new things, from opening up our way of thinking and understanding things. Maybe when you show interest in the way you breathe as if it were the first time ever, you will discover aspects to the phenomenon of breathing that you would never have thought about otherwise. So, already as you experience this without any prejudice, you become richer from the new sensations, new feelings and new emotions that you are feeling. And little by little, sensation by sensation, you are becoming more aware of your breathing, of how you breathe, what comes into play when you do, what is entailed in this process and what that does for you on a physical, perhaps mental (your thoughts, your state of mind, the nature of your thoughts) and emotional level (what you are feeling right now). There is no end to your discovering the way you function and what you are able to do, and discovering all those subtleties that make you who you are.

In fact, you play at listening to yourself, using the body as your intermediary. As you start to listen to yourself without preconceived ideas, judgement or analysis, you develop your capacity for listening. And that's how suddenly in your day-to-day life, you notice that you have fewer preconceptions, you are becoming more open to the outside world and this contributes to your personal development. What is more, now you are more aware that, at times, you may experience a preconceived idea, you have the chance to change your state of mind if you choose to do so.

Without awareness, nothing changes. If you don't want to change anything in your life and if you don't want to change your way of seeing things, then I suggest sophrology isn't for you!

Does sophrology teach us how to breathe?

A sophrology session encourages you to become aware of your breathing as if it were the first time, therefore with no preconceived idea, without prejudice. Even at the tenth time, fiftieth or the thousandth time, you always pretend it is the first time, and you have no expectations. What you do is to experience your breathing consciously, welcoming any sensations, any manifestations, just what is, as it is without judgement or analysis. What you try to do is to live in every moment. This practice helps you become more aware of new sensations, and as you become more and more aware of the way you breathe, you notice how your breathing changes in relation to the physical, psychological and emotional state you are in.

Once you have finally learnt to be aware of how your breathing changes in relation to the state you are in, it means you can now adjust the way you breathe to best respond to the suggestions of the given moment. For example, some people will be aware of the fact that they can't breathe properly when they are concentrated on something or anxious about something. To be aware of this condition means you can take the necessary action in terms of simply allowing yourself time to breathe whenever this situation arises in your day-to-day life. Or you'll try to choose to breathe more deeply, if this is what you need then, or something completely different as you require.

In fact this increase in awareness is the first step, and it is one that will help you make choices regarding your course of action(s), and then to act accordingly.

Without awareness, there is no conscious choice, nor is there positive action. Without awareness, you are passive. And if you are passive, you'll keep ending up in that same state of breathlessness each time you start to worry, and in turn hyperventilating until you end up in that physiological state of stress which will in no way help you psychologically. And so life goes on.

The practice of sophrology develops your capacity for awareness and thanks to this you are able to find what breathing you need. There is no dogma attached and no need for specific techniques, you are able to simply be at ease with the way you breathe.

This can take time but bear in mind that statements like "I don't know how to breathe" or "I am breathing all wrong" among others cause a lot of unnecessary tension(s). If this is how you feel, with sophrology you will have the means to modify your breathing whenever you are not comfortable with it.

It is not up to the sophrologist either to explain how to breathe and although we use some breathing techniques in sophrology, these remain simple and natural. It is up to each of us to experiment continuously with our breathing awareness.

When you live an experience in full awareness, you receive ten times more information than you do when you live an experience thinking of something else. Isn't that obvious? Sophrology makes complete sense!

With practice however, it is possible for someone to do an exercise thinking about something else whilst still being well aware of what is taking place as objectively as they themselves can perceive the experience and not in terms of what others expect or indeed of what is believed others expect or want out of it, or even of what should come out of it...

To get back to breathing or any other phenomenon, it is up to each of us to adapt our behaviour; how we do something, act and think, in accordance with our own needs.

This path that leads to freedom begins with the everyday little things.

What happens in a sophrology session?

An individual session begins with some talking; the client talks and the sophrologist listens.

Next, the practitioner explains how he will run the session, (the sequence of exercises he has chosen) and the exercises themselves.

At the end of the session, when the client is completely 'de-sophronised' or in other words, that they have returned to an ordinary state of wakefulness, the sophrologist invites them to describe any feelings, sensations, or thoughts – if any – experienced during the sophrology session; in short, whatever the client remembers about the session and is willing to talk about. Once again, the practitioner is there just to listen, to allow the client to be even more aware of what was experienced during the session. Then, there is time for the client to ask questions on the technical nature of the exercises.

In a group session, we follow more or less the same process but there is less time available for talking, due to the number of participants. The talking time at the beginning of a session is called the 'pre-sophronic dialogue' and the talking time which follows the practice the 'post-sophronic dialogue'.

At the end of a group session, participants willing to share their experience of the session can do so. Only one other person speaks: the sophrologist, who listens, reformulates if need be, takes into consideration what each participant expresses, without judgement, commentary or analysis. During this time, the other participants remain quiet, continue to listen to their sensations, feelings and thoughts and when one person has finished talking, the next person is free to start.

So, this is not a group discussion about how one person's experience may resonate with what others experienced, nor is it a debate. It is a dialogue between two people: the client and the sophrologist.

What makes group sessions interesting is that whatever the experience of one participant, it may be of considerable significance to the rest, and so it helps everyone to go much further.

What's the point of talking about our experience at the end of a session?

At the end of a session, each person is invited to talk about what they experienced, using the first person singular 'I', as they do so. For example: "I felt that one of my shoulders was higher than the other", or "I felt really tall when I got up", or "I was tired of standing up but I was worried about sitting down and disturbing others if I sat down before the others", or "I was super relaxed after the breathing exercise", or "I found that really long", or "I have never felt so light", etc.

Why use the 'I' form?

The reason is that when we use the 'I' form we refer specifically to the idea of 'self'. Using the 'I' form helps to assert the self as an individual. This does not signify developing 'individualism' but rather 'individuality' or the identity which is specific to each one of us. It also means that we speak for ourselves and that we take responsibility for ourselves.

When all the participants in the group have followed the same exercises, the fact that everyone expresses themselves enables us to realise that everyone's experience was different. This is a very formative experience especially in a group of adolescents or children.

Sometimes, people describe the way they felt and it is similar to the way others felt, but it is also different for others, whether in terms of physical, mental or emotional experience. When a client says he felt very cold during the practice and that this prevented him from concentrating, that the next person to talk describes a very pleasant feeling of freshness all around, and that another brings up his own in contrast to these two experiences and describes a very warm feeling, exactly what he needed to feel right then, we realise that within just one parameter alone, be it that of internal sensations, experiences or perceptions, our physical and emotional feelings can all be very different.

And so you ask: and what if somebody is hot or cold, what difference does it make to say it?

Just saying it is what counts!

If you are at a dinner table or some gathering of sort and you start telling everyone about your physical sensations and your frame of mind you won't interest anybody; in fact you'll probably bore most people. Here however, it doesn't matter what you say, everything you say is respected, accepted without judgement, commentary or interpretation. Beware though: you are not here to tell your life story, but just to talk about what you noticed, what you felt, sensed, thought about during the session.

The feeling of being respected and feeling listened to is a very soothing one. It contributes to your sense of existence and it helps us be more attentive to ourselves. When you talk, everything makes more sense to you because the sophrologist helps you hear what you are saying. When you express yourself **in** this way at the end of each session, it is as though you are placing a jigsaw piece in front of you. Each session produces its own piece and from joining the pieces together, a clearer picture starts to be formed. And so awareness is gained piece by piece.

At times, large pieces of the jigsaw cannot be joined without the inclusion of a small piece at first seemingly in-significant or unimportant in appearance (here referring to something mundane or ordinary that was experienced) but suddenly, the picture gets even clearer. It is as if your awareness is suddenly switched on and with it comes a sense of great satisfaction because what matters is that we come out of that haziness and are able to see clearly and are able move on.

That jigsaw is you!

What if I don't talk at the end of the session?

If occasionally at the end of an individual session you don't want to say anything, it doesn't really matter because after all a well-led sophrology session is valuable enough in itself to allow progress. However, when there is systematic non-participation there will inevitably be something missing from the experience, which although a choice is nevertheless a shame.

Since you know that you are going to have to express yourself at the end you generally pay more attention to what is happening and this helps your concentration. Then, just before you begin talking, you remember what you felt, noticed, observed in your body, so you have something to say! Sharing particularly enables you to notice everything a session brings to you in terms of sensations, both physical and emotional, and it enables you to get to know yourself better and develop more self-control before you start talking.

It also helps you boost your memory. So already you can see how certain mental capacities (no mention here of intellectual capacities) begin to develop as you consciously work on paying attention to our body.

For example, you want to learn to be calmer, so you develop your capacity to calm down when you decide you need to. Just trying to develop this capacity by simply thinking to yourself "I need to feel grounded, I need to feel grounded, I need to feel grounded" isn't going be very effective! And anyway, what does 'feeling grounded' mean? The same goes with 'relaxing'. Maybe you'll manage to relax for 5 minutes during a coffee break, or after a game of squash or while you are watching a cool TV programme. But what happens as soon as the kids need your attention and you are not ready to give it to them, or you have to prepare dinner or go to work, or be in the front line, put up with the noise and all the everyday stress factors?

The practice of sophrology enables you to develop all your mental capacities so that you integrate them not just occasionally, but in a lasting way.

It helps you with your personal ecology: the practice of sophrology activates some parts of our brain that are not used to being activated. New connections between the brain and the rest of the body are created, even between different parts of the brain connected to the neurons at the level of the intestines and the heart.

To come back to what I was saying regarding speaking at the end of a session, when you express yourself, it helps you to take stock, to think things over and then you'll pass on consciously to something else. And you make progress from one session to another.

You can also write a description about what you experienced immediately after the session when it is still fresh in your memory and this is what in sophrology jargon we refer to as 'pheno-description'.

You can say "I don't feel like talking" or "I prefer to keep what I feel to myself" and in doing so, you are making your position clear to the sophrologist, to the group and to yourself. So the fact that you express yourself helps you gain a greater awareness, and bit by bit this leads you to greater self-understanding.

It also allows you to stand back. As people gain confidence (especially in group sophrology) they also learn to listen to others, to respect what others are saying, to respect themselves while noticing that their experience is different to that of others. Therefore sophrology helps us develop both our respect of others and our own self-respect. Little by little we learn to accept others and to accept ourselves just as we are. Progressively, we develop self-acceptance and self-esteem.

This is why it is interesting to do sophrology with school children and if possible in group sessions, for the valuable interaction it brings to all.

What's the point of being 'aware'?

It helps you to take action, to become active, to become the protagonist in your life as opposed to just 'getting on with your life'. The more aware you are, the less you'll just 'get on with your life'. When I teach stretching or how to become more supple, I suggest a posture like for instance standing up with your hands on your thighs, leaning forward to see how far forward you can lean without experiencing pain, finding the right stretching movement for you, the right amount of leaning, all of this requires your ability to listen to your body. So you can find the correct position and feel the stretch, just enough to be able to relax at the same time. This requires being present to the body at that particular moment. If you are not aware, if you are not listening to the sensations in your muscles and joints or elsewhere, then all you end up doing very quickly is to just 'get on with doing' that posture and you'll eventually get bored.

Why?

Because in most cases what we want is to go further, we want to go beyond our ability to just get through things, and then it hurts, so we pull our hands back up our thighs (to continue with my example) but then we find it doesn't work and we judge ourselves; so we try again but it still hurts. So we get discouraged, we tell ourselves that this isn't for us, that we'll never be supple, all the negative and undermining talk that typically goes on inside our head. You can use the analogy of this example for many other events or situations.

What do we have to do to become aware?

To begin with, you must pay attention to your body's sensations, to what you are feeling at any given time (see the paragraph: What is the point of listening to your sensations?). For this you must take the time to put yourself in this mindset, really want to do it and make a conscious decision. If you don't decide to do it, then don't.

To use the stretching example again:

- If you're not careful and take your hands down too quickly, a defence mechanism will operate and your muscles will instinctively contract. As a result, you'll experience pain and you'll gain no suppleness since muscular relaxation is needed in order for you to become supple.
- If on the other hand, you decide to take the time to listen to your body's sensations, you may be able to feel which areas are being stretched, to what extent

you can continue stretching without experiencing pain, you will be able to take notice of any unnecessary tensions, and relax as you know how far you can relax. You'll be able to find the right balance between those tensions you need and those that are unnecessary, you'll be aware of your points of contact in order to improve your position, be able to spread your weight equally, feel how you are breathing and maybe even, if this is of interest, make a note of how you feel mentally and emotionally: do you want to push yourself any further? You can even compare with your previous achievements, compare with others, note down everything that's an impediment to your living in the objectivity of the moment and simply welcome what is, right now, your reality.

To be aware is to be here, in the present moment, with your perceptions, your sensations, your thoughts, your feelings in the moment. It is to be in the simplicity of the moment and to really live in the moment. It is the opposite of just getting on with life and getting on with it mechanically.

At this point in time, no matter how you are placed as you are reading these lines, you are placed somewhere aren't you? Well, you are not floating in the air, are you? But are you even aware of how you are placed?

Maybe this question has awakened your interest now that I have mentioned it, so yes, you are becoming aware of it. Can you feel your points of contact? All the different points of contact your body has in the position you're in right now? What is supporting your weight? What sensations do you get from these points of contact? Do they feel warm, cold, hard, soft or rough?

Are you even aware of the way your body is placed? Once you start this awareness game you may start to notice some changes taking place in your body, something changing in your muscular tensions, in the way your body feels, the way your mind feels, your mood, right there at any given moment. And it may be that this in turn brings new sensations and feelings of awareness.

I often read in magazines or hear on the radio or in doctors' surgeries that we must learn 'to be more grounded'.

But how do you do that?

Well, you start at the beginning: by becoming aware of how you are placed, by bringing awareness to your points of contact and the sensations that this brings you. By gaining awareness you reach simplicity. Your day-to-day life is teaming with opportunities so you can listen in to how you feel if only you want to and if you take the time to. When you are aware of being grounded, you develop your mental capacity for becoming more grounded, at will.

As we have seen, the simple fact of being aware of our points of contact makes us more grounded physically first, and then mentally. Our mind quietens, becomes clearer, and this can even be reflected in the sound of our voice as it too calms down.

To start with, it is through your body that you gain awareness. Then you learn to be in touch with your thoughts, your state of mind, and your internal dialogues. You also gain awareness of your feelings, of how you feel emotionally, whatever you are feeling at a given time. Your self-awareness becomes more precise, more diverse and deeper.

Isn't all this a rather self-centred journey?

To be interested in yourself doesn't mean you are only interested in yourself.

But charity begins at home. In truth, you can't take care of others if you don't know how to take a care of yourself, at least a little. If you don't, you'll only bring all your problems to those you are pretending to help.

When you develop your awareness, you become aware of everything around you that shapes you and shapes the world too. It makes you more sensitive, more emotionally intelligent (that famous E.Q.) and it leads you bit by bit – when you've worked hard on yourself – to full awareness.

You sense and you feel more intensely what takes place inside of you but also what takes place in others thanks to the fact that you activate your capacities of non-judgement and non-interpretation and are therefore more connected on a self-to-self basis. To sum it up, practising sophrology and meditation overall develops your capacity for compassion and empathy.

How come being more aware makes us more active?

When you take part in my class and you put yourself in your chosen position, making the necessary adjustments, you use the different parameters – angles, self-judgement, breathing, etc – that are necessary until you find the position and all the sensations that go with it that suit you. So you are proactive in your search for wellbeing. The opposite to someone who takes action is someone who doesn't take the time to listen in to their feelings, gets hurt, endures the pain and ends up having to react to the situation. That is where the notion of choice has come in.

How often in life, do you say: "I don't have a choice" and how often do you hear this negative claim? It is true that sometimes there is little choice, but there is still a choice. It is simply that you are not aware of the choices that are available to you. And so you continue to endure the situation.

As a participant to my stretching class you can either choose to lean a little more forward and still a little more; you can choose to move faster, you can stop from time to time to be more aware of any sensations; you can use all your energy in one go or choose to leave something in reserve; you can be partially or completely relaxed; you can breathe slowly, deeply, fix your attention to the inhalation or the exhalation to sense the differences... there is no end to the amount of choices you have once you decide to start to listen in.

And it is up to you to make your choice or choices and to act accordingly. Once you are aware of the range of choices available to you, it's up to you to make your selection and when and how to take action. That's what we call acting with complete awareness. If when carrying out a stretching exercise, you decide to adopt that painful position, it is your choice: you don't have to endure it if you are acting with true awareness, according to the choices you've made.

That is your responsibility.

How long before I get better? When do I see results and start to feel well?

This is a question people systematically ask at the beginning of their journey.

In fact, from the first session onward, you can feel the beneficial physical, mental or emotional adjustments that take place. However, since the sessions follow on from one another and your experience each time is different – remember you are in a phenomenological state of mind – it may be that you feel more tense, experience some pain during or after, or that you feel no sensation at all at the following session and then you feel amazing the next, and so it goes on!

What does 'feeling well' mean?

Does it mean being without stress, being relaxed and pain free?

Does it mean sleeping all the time?

To be calm and free from worries?

To be able to cope with everything, to be Zen?

Of course that depends on each person. Some people will very quickly feel the benefits from sophrology whereas others will need longer.

In fact, it depends on your ability to expect nothing, just take an interest in what is happening at any time during a session and allow the learning to take place. Becoming aware that you are resisting physically and mentally, aware of tensions when you judge, analyse or expect something to happen – concrete results or something extraordinary – realising that you haven't let go of prejudices, and that you are holding yourself back from discovering new things, are all big steps that will enable you to later let go and to live what there is to live in your life in the present moment.

Just being aware that you are resisting, simply noticing that this is what you are doing, without judging yourself allows you, in one way or another, to progress towards wellbeing, self-respect, and self-acceptance.

When you begin to identify what it is that you are resisting, you see more clearly how you function within, and you can learn to act according to what you really need.

Little by little you begin to blossom, and then there is no stopping.

No one can predict how long it will take for you to feel better!

This also depends on your environment, on how often you practise, what you do in your training and how much you invest in yourself, how much confidence you have in the method and in your sophrologist...

It is a bit like when you go to a supermarket to shop. You are quite set on buying bread, milk and jam. Then as you browse through the shelves you find offers on strawberries and green beans, you pass by the pet food aisle and you remember that you have no cat food left, and from one aisle to the next you fill your trolley with a load of other things that you had not intended to buy when you started. You need all of that too but you had not thought about any of it when you started.

When you are working on yourself, particularly in sophrology, it is the same thing: you come up with an idea that maybe you'll get some relief for a particular pain or worry or for stress, then you discover something you had not even thought about. You develop new abilities, discover new potential; you come across some really useful techniques; learn new ideas... and before long you probably notice that you are feeling better in different ways. Often, before you can find relief for the things that preoccupy you, it is probably necessary to release, improve or review some aspects of your life you were not even thinking about.

You may or may not necessarily get better straight away and what you'll experience will without a doubt be different to what you'd hoped or expected.

Your journey may take you on some tortuous, surprising and unexpected paths, for the unconscious works in mysterious ways!

Can sophrology cure me from insomnia?

Both in my groups and individual sessions I have clients who come because they want to sleep better and they only end up sleeping better after they have done one year of sophrology; others come to me for completely different reasons and, two weeks later, they tell me that they have been sleeping like a baby since they started practising sophrology!

What is certain is that you are going to learn techniques that will allow you to focus, to rest, to relax, to let go physically, mentally and emotionally and this will be beneficial in helping you go to sleep and going back to sleep if you wake up during the night. You will gain in autonomy.

You will learn to know yourself better, to take notice of the way you function and what is beneficial for you. You will do this in a more objective and therefore in a more efficient manner.

You will develop your capacity to put things in perspective, to live in the present moment and not to anticipate the following day with negative thoughts. When you can't sleep, the danger is in wanting to sleep so that you feel good the following day and be able to take care of all the tasks that need your attention. Just thinking about it causes stress and that prevents you from sleeping even more. It causes annoyance or worry and, with this deficit of sleep, you get up in the morning probably feeling tense, shattered and in a bad mood.

With sophrology you will learn how to conserve energy better and therefore manage your time, tasks and situations even if you've only had a little sleep – a very useful thing to be able to do in many jobs including that of parenting! Just by simply not trying to get to sleep and simply welcoming your sensations, being aware of your points of contact on the bed for example, the sensations of softness that the sheets or the quilt provide, feeling your breath or concentrating on a neutral object – a contemplation technique used in the first level of relaxation – can all help you relax, stop you focusing on your insomnia and its consequences and thus waste less energy in trying to get to sleep. You may get to sleep and if you don't, you'll at least feel more rested when you get up and more empowered to deal with the day ahead. It's the feeling of being powerless to do anything that's very stressful.

In fact, the practice of sophrology brings new balance into our lives and little by little this has the effect of improving sleep, making it more beneficial. Periods of insomnia get shorter and shorter, and less frequent over time.

Many sailors use sophrology in order to manage their lack of sleep, tiredness and even to 'program themselves' to be able to sleep at a given time. You need to have a minimum amount of self-awareness to be able to do this and that is precisely what sophrology is about. And so the circle is complete.

But in all honesty, the same goes with the practice of yoga, chi gong, hypnosis, E.F.T., Reiki and any other method aiming to get rid of physical, emotional and mental tensions, to help focus better and rebalance our energies. It is up to each one of us to find what suits us best in our life, when we need it.

What's the recommended number of weekly sessions?

Apart from the weekly session in a group or on an individual basis, ideally, this should be practised daily, either through a repeat of the whole session or chosen sections.

It is up to each of us to find the rhythm that is right for us in terms of our own capacities and our timetable.

Yes, BUT, it isn't the same at home as it is in a session with a sophrologist

Of course not; it is more difficult when we are alone but it isn't impossible, it is just different. What we have to do is to decide to do it. You may have to make yourself find the time, give yourself a little push, like with anything else new at the beginning, but it is important to get started. Of course, you don't have the guiding voice of the sophrologist but this is prerequisite to becoming autonomous.

The choice is yours...

Do you sometimes eat out? Sometimes it's different, sometimes it's better than eating at home and most of all, it's relaxing but that doesn't stop you from eating at home! Ultimately where you eat is of no consequence because feeding yourself is vital. Similarly it is possible to make the daily practice of sophrology to your taste, to tailor-make your practice so that it brings the necessary vital nourishment to your physical, intellectual and emotional life enabling you to move forwards and grow.

What's the best time of the day to practise?

It doesn't matter. Since this is like an experiment, you'll test this for yourself and decide when it's best for you, and you may find that mornings are more conducive, or the middle of the day or the evening before bedtime. And it may even change from week to week. And you may just feel like practising it at any given time, just because you feel like practising!

Ideally, there should be a minimum amount of discipline involved. As one of my colleagues who was a yoga teacher often used to say to me: "Pleasure comes with discipline and practice."

You can also programme a timetable of appointments with yourself. Sometimes people don't practise because they say they are afraid they will be disturbed and because of that they can't relax. When you have an appointment with your doctor or someone else, you get there and you don't ask yourself if you are going to be disturbed, so you can do the same if you arrange an appointment with yourself.

Try to make sure you don't get disturbed, organise yourself and respect your commitment to yourself as if it were a specialist that you had an appointment with.

Where should I practise?

In a quiet place, where you feel comfortable is best. Generally though keep things simple. You shouldn't practise when you are annoyed, tired or stressed. You'd be better off going out for a run, doing Zumba, making pancakes or having a bath!

The main reason you should train is to fully assimilate the new skills and techniques learned with your sophrologist. The acquisition of these techniques will enable you to manage your day-to-day tasks, relationships and situations to the very best of your ability. As with any new activity, it is important to do it in an environment where we feel safe, in a place that is both adequate and pleasant. Don't make things difficult for yourself or you'll get discouraged and you'll probably fail in your attempts to practise on your own.

To use the analogy of football: a player doesn't, on the day of his match, arrive on the pitch without having first worked on the physical abilities required of him. Whether it is endurance, resistance, focus, power, flexibility, adaptability, reflexes or his skills of concentration, anticipation and analysis, he will have gone through all the necessary training in the most suitable surroundings possible.

Then, gradually, as you start to feel something is working, something is changing somewhere within, you can experiment – sophrology is an experiment – in surroundings that are more challenging. For example, in a noisy or busy environment, in the street, waiting for a train, in a waiting room, etc.

In as much as sophrology is the study of all elements of consciousness in harmony, the development of self-awareness, of our capacities and human values becomes a constant presence in our life.

To be aware means to be present to what we are doing, saying, feeling and thinking about: about the way we act, what is going on inside us, and around us.

The goal is to be aware on a day-to-day basis, and for this, we need to think about what we do as we do it.

For example, when you are driving, it is a good idea to be present to your driving, and be aware of what you are doing otherwise you might brake too late because you didn't see the car in front of you slow down, or you might drive past the motorway exit and end up adding another twenty or thirty miles to your journey. And so it goes on.

What does it mean: to 'work on ourselves'?

People often tell me that they don't need to do sophrology because they know how to relax, they are not stressed, they know how to manage things and get on with them, etc. and it is true, some people manage quite well for themselves.

However, something doesn't quite ring true here. There is something missing.

So I ask myself: what if we could sum up that 'missing something' as honesty?

To be honest with ourselves, not telling lies to ourselves.

And what if all this 'gaining awareness' work means that what we do is to work on ourselves and ask questions about ourselves?

And what if becoming honest means having to automatically go through this gaining of awareness that in turns leads to a better understanding of ourselves and of human nature?

In my opinion to 'work on ourselves' means that we learn to be honest with ourselves, in every respect, in every way.

It may be that we begin by recognising our qualities and our faults and by asking ourselves if our body, head and heart are working together in harmony, free from conflict. It may also mean admitting to ourselves how we really feel deep down about things.

Lying to ourselves inevitably leads to disagreements and to internal conflict. This in turn leads to discomfort, pain, disease of all sorts, insomnia, and depression...

How many times do we lie to ourselves in the course of a day without even realising or perhaps, on the contrary, in denial of the fact that we do?

Here are some typical examples:

- We say we don't deserve to be praised for something we did even though we tell ourselves deep down that we think we did really well.

- We pretend to ourselves that we don't hold anything against someone when deep down our anger simmers and grows until it manifests itself in the way we talk and react – often inappropriately since we are not aware of what we are really experiencing within.

- We make ourselves believe a situation is normal even though in our body we feel actual physical pain.

- We want what someone else has despite the fact we know it isn't really for us.

Our existence is made up of and layered with false beliefs that we hold about ourselves; some we created ourselves, others were contributed to by our environment.

To become aware of what we believe, how our body works, how we feel and think about things is what enables us to work on our honesty. Such awareness helps us recognise and respect our limits, and to move forward towards greater harmony and balance.

We gain in simplicity, in respect and acceptance of who we are, in lightness of being, in clarity, in self-esteem, and in self-love.

And this has an effect on others. Since we feel better about ourselves, we are better around others and we feel less fearful.

Sometimes the reason we feel fearful in a relationship is because we don't want to get hurt. We are fearful that another may touch something within us, something that is fragile in us.

Once we've become aware of our own faults, our fragility, our lack of ease in a situation or this lack of whatever it is that we've admitted to in all honesty. Once we stop pretending that it's all in our imagination or that it is somebody else's fault, when we respect our fragility, this Achilles heel, accepting it as it is, then we reach the stage when no one can get to us any longer.

It hurts when something touches that hidden part of ourselves, that which we guard and/or ignore by means of carefully maintained resistance.

The result is often our resisting that other person even though the source of the problem isn't them.

Thus we create conflict internally with our head, body and heart, as well as conflict externally with others.

When we are honest with ourselves we are able to let go, we gain the freedom needed to understand ourselves better. Paradoxically, when we recognise what is within us, that 'something' which is within us doesn't in fact gain in strength, rather it becomes part of the process towards finding inner peace. We are thus more able to lay certain expectations to rest. For example wanting to be slimmer, be better at some subject or other or be able to discover something new and wonderful! As we turn the page and learn to let go and accept things as they are, something changes within us; there is a subtle shift that leads to a deeper sense of peace and harmony.

Meditation helps us reconnect with ourselves, with our source, with our inner self, our true self and to develop our awareness.

Sophrology works in the same way.

In fact, if you are doing sophrology and psychotherapy at the same time, you'll find the latter to be more effectively beneficial and faster. Both help you in your search for honesty with yourself and both help you understand more clearly how you process things.

Why practise standing rather than lying down?

The aim of sophrology is to develop awareness and for that to happen it is appropriate to remain awake. The lying down position is likely to encourage you to sleep. It's not that unusual for people to go to sleep when they are sitting down, let alone if they are lying down. If you fall asleep it isn't a problem, but when you've missed half of the session it is like falling asleep at the cinema; what a waste!

What is more, the vertical positions, whether standing or sitting, are more dynamic as far as the body is concerned and when we train in this vertical position we develop our capacity for switching off, resting, relaxing, becoming self-aware and living in the present moment whether doing the washing-up, sitting at the dinner table, the office, in a car, while waiting at the till, working in a shop, doing sport, or in any situations.

When you are balanced, anchored, upright with your feet on the ground, it all contributes to your level of confidence.

In my work with children in various schools and community setups over the course of a decade or so, I noticed that when I guided them to become more body aware, aware of their contact with the ground, of their verticality, etc. they would rapidly gain in assurance. They would not only stand better but they would take a stand in relation to others both in the figurative and the proper sense of the word. Some mums would say to me: "I don't know what it is you do, but my daughter is singing at home now, she is more cheerful and she is feeling good enough about herself to ask for things directly without whinging or complaining" or "my son is calmer, he doesn't get annoyed at the slightest thing anymore, and he takes more time to explain how he feels". These are just two examples among many.

The practice of sophrology in the vertical position develops our ability to manage our muscular tensions, be aware of our points of contact and the distribution of our body weight, of the effects of gravity, of our posture and the right balance we need for ourselves...

What is more, the reasons for adopting a vertical position are not just physical. As explained earlier, the impact is also mental and emotional especially when it comes to children. We just don't feel the same when we are lying down or when we are slumped as opposed to sitting with our back straight; neither does it feel the same when we are standing lopsided or twisted rather than up straight.

Our state of mind isn't the same. So our very posture does impact our state of mind and our state of mind does impact the way we sit or stand. It's both a physical and a mental thing.

Practising sophrology in a vertical position contributes to the development of harmonious self-awareness; we become more connected in relation to our self, our body, our needs, our hopes and our values.

Once we are connected, we can become ourselves.

Do we never practise sophrology lying down?

Of course we do in certain situations for example if someone is not able to remain seated or if someone is bedridden or in hospital. It is mostly on a one-to-one session, but inasmuch as it is possible depending on the state of health of the client, we practise in a vertical position.

The importance of the discourse

During a sophrology session the sophrologist's voice predominates, using a very specific wording, tone and rhythm that we call the 'terpnos logos' – the word comes from the Greek and means 'discourse/words'. The sophrologist guides but does not impose or induce any concrete images or sensations as the idea is for everyone else participating to experience whatever they are 'meant' to experience at that particular moment, whatever it is. This involves a very conscious effort on the part of the sophrologist who is only too aware that their choice of words, turns of phrase, sentence length, pauses and intonation, all have an impact.

The guiding must also be powerful enough to 'hit our consciousness' as Bernard Santerre, founder and former director of the Sophrology Institute in Rennes, (who died in August 2011) would say.

Achieving this specific guiding technique requires the sophrology student to practise and experiment with the choice of words and tone, etc. Students are encouraged to meet other students and test their choice of talking technique. Students undertake rigorous training and work hard on themselves to gain in awareness so that they become able to adjust their wording to optimise the fluency and relevance of their sessions.

In the course of a visualisation, the sophrologist doesn't tell you what to see, hear, smell, sense, feel or perceive. This is particularly true in group sessions where each person has their own experience. Visualisations are however quite specific and tailor-made for the session and used with care by the professional who is guiding. At a level of modified consciousness, the words, rhythms and the sound frequencies all impact on the psyche of those being guided and therefore the discourse used has to be created with great care.

What will practising sophrology do for me?

Practising sophrology allows you to develop your mental faculties, your full potential and the capacities you have within. These may be latent, not used to their best or used inappropriately. Sophrology can thus help you to fully realise yourself as an individual, total awareness of your abilities and of the choices you have, so you can live in harmony, as much as is possible, free from conflict with yourself, your environment, your past, present and future. This is in part thanks to the capacity for self-confidence that sophrology develops.

When you practise sophrology your brain works to encourage the creation of new connections and synapses and the ensuing beneficial effects can be observed in the cortex as much as in the limbic and the reptilian brains.

The sophrology participant develops a much greater awareness of their body and discovers new mental capacities that are in fact already within but which so far have been little explored or even neglected, and these now develop and become stronger.

Specific exercises reinforce our capacity for concentration, our capacity for being in the moment, encouraging us to be focused and aware of how we feel physically, mentally and emotionally.

What is more, someone who practises sophrology notices that their level of intuition improves and this is especially thanks to the work we do on developing our awareness of the senses, always in a phenomenological way without any preconceived ideas and as if it were for the first time.

We also develop our capacity for decision-making. Choices have to be made, but we don't need to load our intellect with endless questions anymore; rather, we ask the right questions, and we think efficiently, without time-wasting.

Someone who practises sophrology also notices that as they learn to be without prejudice their curiosity develops as does their capacity to wonder at the world around them, to learn and to always be open to new things – not be blasé or bitter. They develop their ability to welcome everything as though it were the first time, without judgement.

Equally, we develop inner honesty, understanding of and respect for others, empathy, moderation, a non-judgemental attitude towards ourselves and others and the ability to refrain from jumping to conclusions.

What is noticeable in the course of a group session is that despite everyone seemingly having taken part in that same session, when it comes to each person describing their experience, it is clear that practically nobody has experienced the same thing.

While one person speaks, the rest remain silent and no one intervenes to make comments or give advice or worse still pass judgement. The only dialogue that takes place is purely between the sophrologist and the participant. In this way, everyone can express themselves freely about their experience of the session and this allows everyone to be aware that despite appearances, everyone's experience is different.

Sophrology of course helps with physical relaxation, to quieten and empty the mind and see things in a different way.

As our brain drops down to the alpha wave level, we become less vigilant and our mind no longer analyses logically. Instead, it makes analogies: sometimes, through the sensations and various feelings experienced, a client is able to make links that they could not have made in an ordinary state of wakefulness. It isn't unusual for people to tell me they've found the solution to an ongoing issue in the course of their sophrology session.

The practice of sophrology develops all the positive aspects of a person. It is great in terms of its preventative function in that when we are faced with worries or problems we feel much more resilient having worked on recognising our emotions, what is happening in our head and in our body. Sophrology puts at our disposal some much reinforced capacities such as the capacity for stepping back, for seeing things as they are rather than as we imagine them to be or as we think they ought to be.

Sophrology teaches us how to control our breathing and our physical symptoms of stress so that we recognise them in time to know what to do; we can quickly calm ourselves down and put ourselves back on track, we can face reality without letting it affect us, and we can thus make the best possible choices. We learn how to take our responsibilities on board while respecting ourselves fully. Learning to understand ourselves better is imminently formative.

Bernard Santerre, aforementioned, used to say that sophrology was the "teaching of existence" and I totally agree with him.

As far as I am concerned, I've learned more in one year of sophrology than I have in ten years of my life and as I haven't stopped learning since then, that learning has become exponential.

The more you are aware, the more you become aware.

Let me use the following for an image: there is a tree in front of you, you can see the trunk, then its branches, and there are twigs on the branches, and then there are leaves on the twigs of the branches…

So, yes of course sophrology is for everyone! Those who come to my classes say that if they had known about it sooner, they may have avoided an awful lot of problems. They also say that sophrology should be taught in schools. Well, yes… let it be said loud and clear!

The development of human consciousness is a major concern of our times. There are lots of methods involved in this area of interest and sophrology is only one of them, but it is a simple, fast and accessible method that anyone can use. All you need is the willingness to do it, and to also want humankind to progress to a more humane way of living and of life. This is truly a project of a political nature, but is not the object of my work, at least not in this book!

What's a sensation? What is it we have to feel?

In a sophrology session you listen to your sensations in the present moment. Some people often say that they don't feel anything and they wonder what it is they ought to feel.

You don't have to feel anything in particular; it is just about you taking the time to listen in to your body, to your sensations whatever they may be.

Yes, but… what do you call 'a sensation'?

A sensation is what we sense, it's the information, the message that we receive or that we perceive.

It can be anything. For example, the contact of your feet in your shoes, the contact of your back against the chair, the movements in your belly as you breathe in and out, the air circulating through your nose, the sensation caused by the bracelet on your wrist. The contact of your clothing with your arm, a gurgling sound in your tummy, how your jaw feels when you yawn, the position of your right hand at a given time, some muscular tension in your shoulder, an itchy nostril, in short anything that you are able to notice for yourself at a given time.

Note that as I said previously, it isn't up to the sophrologist to induce a sensation. For instance a sophrologist will simply ask you to listen in to your sensations, to be mindful of your sensations, whatever and wherever they are, on your face for example. You may notice some tingling, maybe a sensation of coolness, of imbalance between the two sides of your body, the sensation of the air around you or of your hair on your forehead, the sensation of the presence of your eyes in their socket or the shape of your nose… to name but a few. There is an infinite number of sensations you may feel and in sophrology none brings any value judgement with it at all.

Everything is of interest and anything you sense is there to allow you to gain awareness of your body reality, not just in terms of any pains or body dysfunctions. Sensations may be unpleasant, they can also be pleasant or just neutral.

We don't judge; all we do is take notice.

In any case, it isn't up to the sophrologist to tell you that your forehead is warm or that it's cold, or to tell you that you can feel your face relaxing. These would be inferences or induced sensations and the risk is that if you don't feel that what the sophrologist is telling you applies to you, then you may feel that you are not getting anywhere. Inductions are reserved for other quite specific methods such as hypnosis where they are used with a particular therapeutic goal and are certainly not improvised. It is like with any of the great arts: an artist is at liberty to improvise once he is in full control of his tools and his method. For a therapist, this means having acquired the know-how, and having worked on himself.

One of the sophrologist's difficulties and one of their talents is precisely that of teaching others how to use the tools and the work method as autonomously as possible. This is so that the client is free to discover themselves at their own pace.

Of course, for a sophrologist to never induce anything is not just difficult but practically impossible because if only through the use of their voice, the sophrologist automatically induces a lower or a higher level of wakefulness depending on the tone, range, rhythm that they adopt. However it is part of the sophrologist's job to be fully aware of what they say and do at any point of a sophrology session. They must constantly work on themselves too in order to refine their discourse, to refine the words used during the session and how they use them.

The discourse, that is to say the 'terpnos logos' is an integral and vital part of any sophrology session as participants are in modified levels of alertness.

At this point I feel I should mention that, sometimes, teachers (of PE, yoga, drama or else) claim to do sophrology at the end of a lesson. Even though it may often be something very pleasant and very relaxing and participants may love it, what they do is not sophrology.

It is important not to misuse the term 'sophrology' even if using the word is likely to bring it coverage and contribute to its integration in our everyday life and language. To become a sophrologist requires thorough and specialised training; sophrology isn't something that can be improvised as is true of all other physical and mental disciplines. I am talking about professions in their own right.

To be honest, what is important in my opinion is to really explain what we do. When we use relaxation tools in the course of, or at the end of a class, we tell people what we are doing and we know what it is we are doing.

It is out of respect for the professionals who were trained properly and who are experts in their field that we must do this, out of respect for the teachers and especially out of respect for the public who trust in the method.

Without wanting to preach morality I do wonder what happens when a teacher uses a visualisation with no knowledge of its causes and effects and a student runs out of his class very upset? If you have any questions relating to this sort of scenario don't hesitate to contact me. Enough of that! I've now said what I had to say.

So what is it we must sense?

Well, nothing special in fact: we often look for, or expect particular sensations that are out of the ordinary or even extraordinary. But in fact all this is about is to sense how we connect to the ordinary, to the everyday things like those already mentioned among so many other possibilities, those things which we never really pay attention to because we don't take the time to, or judge the exercise to be pointless and nonsensical.

And once we've learned to make time, to allow ourselves time to listen to all those ordinary little things, at last our capacity for feeling and welcoming other sensations that we never suspected existed, becomes more refined and grows.

And this is how, one step at a time and without shouting it from the roof tops, we quite simply and progressively set foot on this path we call self-awareness.

Little by little, everything becomes interesting and we also learn to listen in to our thoughts, our mind chatter, our states of mind, our feelings and how we feel on the inside.

And little by little, without making any value judgement, and with no preconceived ideas or particular expectations, we come to understand more and more what is happening inside of us.

And thus we start living our life more intensely and more and more consciously all the time, becoming more and more aware of our own existence; feeling alive. Everything becomes a source of interest or even curiosity, astonishment and wonder.

What do you recommend: one-to-one or group sessions?

That really depends on your individual preference.

What's important is that you feel comfortable. Some people prefer the intimacy and confidentiality of a one-to-one session while others are interested in, or feel the need to be in a group session.

In a one-to-one, it is easier for you to express yourself in relation to your personal issues, to your life. The sophrologist can also target the work they do according to the needs expressed by their client.

In a group, what is said by any of the participants can resonate with others and help them think about aspects they hadn't thought about before; or they may, thanks to the sophrologist's ability to actively listen, find help in partly resolving their own issues. The group creates a certain energy and brings a dynamic to the growth of awareness of each participant. In a group, you learn to express yourself in public, you learn be more assertive, to respect and recognise yourself and others alike and how they resemble or differ from you. Working as a group contributes to you finding your place in life, in the world. What's more, since group sessions are cheaper, people can pursue sophrology for longer and therefore they can make more progress.

For my part, I always ask that those clients of mine who come to me individually follow up with group sophrology sessions as soon as they feel ready to do so. Likewise, those who practise group sophrology can benefit from one-to-one sessions as and when the need arises for them.

The notion of confidentiality

Sophrologists are obviously bound by professional secrecy so none of what is discussed in the course of any of the one-to-one or group sessions is revealed outside. The same applies for all the group participants. Everyone must respect confidentiality. This is crucial if trust is to be established and it is something that needs to be explained at the beginning of the sessions.

How can moving my shoulders up and down help me get more out of life?

If you move your shoulders up and down – a dynamic exercise found in first level of sophrology – while you think about something else without paying attention to what you are doing, it won't get you very far.

On the other hand, if you shake your shoulders about and you live this movement as though it were a new experience, paying attention to what you are doing, the sensations you are feeling, the choices you are making as you are dealing with the stimulation – for example, the intensity, the duration of the movement, its speed etc. -, then that changes everything.

Once you actively participate in your life, one result is that you realise what is happening in your body.

The time for a pause that follows the dynamic exercises is useful for you to integrate better and as mindfully as possible all the information that is passing through you; all those physical, mental and emotional signs that the stimulation has triggered in you. It serves, if only on a physical level, to make you aware of what the movement involved. All of this takes place in the spirit of phenomenology, with no expectation, judgement or analysis. We welcome nothing but the information we are about to store in this databank of ours, those jigsaw pieces which will later fit together all by themselves.

We don't make connections, they just happen by themselves. However, the more information we store about ourselves, the greater the number of these connections, and the greater our awareness.

The greater our awareness, the better we know how to live our life actively rather than in a passive way. In fact, the shoulder exercise, like any other sophrology dynamic relaxation exercise, enables us to better connect with our body so we can experience it more mindfully and develop our capacity for listening, for just welcoming whatever is happening at any given moment and be more objective.

When we develop our own self-awareness, we develop our capacity to take positive action in our life and therefore to use our creativity.

So as you can see, there is a lot more to just moving our shoulders up and down!

And what if we can't move our shoulders or do any other exercise?

You can imagine that you are doing it. This will trigger in your brain the same phenomenon albeit with less intensity. You can also listen in to sense how not being able to do the exercise feels. You must always do this without commentary or judgement, otherwise no changes will take place.

It is interesting to note how much your capacity for objectivity – among other capacities special to each one of us at a given time – develops, just through observing.

What happens next? What is it meant to do for me?

Sometimes, people tell me that they can't see what one particular exercise or another does for them, they can't see the point in it, they don't understand the method, they feel blocked, and they wonder what is the point in them being here.

That happens to all of us, it has happened and it will continue to happen, if not with respect to sophrology, with other things, with other training.

In fact, we function backwards. We want to grasp everything, we want to get results quickly, before we've even taken the time to experiment. And for as long as we function in this way, then we get frustrated and we don't pursue anything to the end.

As I've said many times, the secret lies in not expecting anything. The more we expect it to do something for us, the less we will sense what is happening in us. With expectation, comes stress that prevents us from being receptive, open to ourselves and to everything that could happen; things could be happening but we are not capable of feeling them or tapping into them consciously at that moment in time.

Generally, when someone says "I can't see what this is doing for me" it is because they are expecting something special, something new, or extraordinary, something better or an added something. Once more, when we are in this state of stress expecting something to happen, we'll feel nothing or, worse, we may become aware of some increased pain.

Indeed at the beginning, we often only feel strong sensations which frequently come in the form of pain, although not always. On the other hand, the sessions have such a very relaxing effect that the level of wakefulness drops very close to that of sleep which can be very pleasing for some but border on the frustrating for others: "Okay, and what now?" they ask.

In fact, what we can do is to welcome the little child that is in us, with that capacity that children have to experiment with things, to be curious, without any preconceived ideas or judgement, to feel wonderment.

Already in utero, the experiences of a foetus are of a sensorial nature. From birth and for the first three years of life, there is no end to that experiencing: touching, tasting – anything and everything! – touching while tasting since the sense of touch is very developed in and around the mouth, smell, watching, examining more closely and listening.

Everything is new and every bit of life is full of valuable learning and information. From all these sensorial experiences, new sensations accumulate that are linked to touch, taste, sight, smell and hearing.

And with all this checking of sensations and the accumulation of other information, a child gains a certain awareness, notices new things happening and in the end understands their function.

It is thanks to those experiences which are far from insignificant – only interpreted as such by adults unaware of their function – that the brain constructs itself.

It is generally through sensorial and physical experiences that intelligence develops. What a child learns between the age of zero and three is phenomenal. Why not observe them and learn again with them?

Later, when we grow up, we are less and less in the simple, sensorial, everyday body experience. We know everything so we take it for granted and we keep looking for stronger sensations in order to feel we exist, to feel pleasure in existing. And what's more, we want to understand everything before we experience it. Our intellect takes over our experiencing and it takes over our body.

As we develop our ability to experience as if it were the first time in the same way as a small child does – even though we know it isn't the case – our brain continues to grow and makes new connections, synapses between the different brain regions and the rest of our body, glial cells and neurons. The very awareness that we have of ourselves and the outside world continues to grow.

Thanks to the work we do on our senses, which is very important in sophrology, we gain a greater awareness of our relationship with the outside world and our existence, thanks to simple little things close to hand (or our eyes or ears!) Our day-to-day experience becomes more and more sensory and we take pleasure in existing.

A small child does all of that without thinking; it is part of his growing up. When an adult in Western society has forgotten how to be like the small child, sophrology can help them carry on experiencing things consciously, which in turn impacts their experience of the here and now.

This happens little by little, not all at once, straight away, or right now! The fact that we let go in terms of our intellect and our expectations – without preconceived ideas or analysis – and we take an interest in what we do without judging, enables us to live our body experiences fully and this includes our mental and emotional sensations as they are manifested throughout our body. As we continue to allow ourselves to welcome experiences, we continue gathering new and varied sensations that inform us of what we are living physically, mentally and emotionally, in the present moment. And as we continue to integrate this information, we become more aware of how we function, and this in turn leads us to understand ourselves as people and as human beings.

This is why if we don't leave the door open, without any expectations, we cannot see how sophrology can be of benefit to us.

We won't know what benefits it can bring us either if we don't get to work and take things reasonably seriously with a minimum amount of self-discipline.

In fact, so we can understand things better it would be better to ask: "What will sophrology teach me?"

The previous question had implied a certain passivity: that of a consumer expecting it all to come from the method. However, nothing happens as long as we remain in this passive state of mind, and so we learn nothing.

Now that we've turned the question around and that we ask "what will sophrology teach me?", the premise of the question is that I am ready to allow learning to take place. The question shows commitment and humility.

And now the session is neither going to be a good one or a bad one; it will simply be interesting, because there will always be something to be learnt, if only about how we function inside. For example, noticing that we are waiting for something in particular to manifest itself...

When we do sophrology we take an active role, not a passive or a consumerist role.

I can't manage to concentrate, how can I improve this?

Here is another of those recurring questions.

When you concentrate, you are interested. It would be interesting to ask ourselves if we are really interested in what we are doing during a session. And when people tell me that they have "parasitic thoughts" or that they tend to "get into their own world", it is because most of the time, they don't value what they are living in the present moment enough, not really or concretely. When I question them on the subject, their answer is that they are not really that interested; they can't see what it is doing for them.

They are more interested in their problems or in their day-to-day business, in what the future holds for them or what happened in their past even if that was a very short while ago. And so, they take no interest in what they are experiencing. They are interested in what they experienced or what they may experience in the future, but not in what they are experiencing right now.

Once again, it is a choice. It is up to each one of us to choose to be interested in what we are experiencing here and now, in other words, to be present or not, as the case may be. No one can do this for us.

What's the point of living in the present moment?

The point is, rather, not always being in the past or in the future!

To be right there, alive, complete, with a body, with a head and with a heart.

Have you ever had to face someone lost in their own thoughts over a dinner? You were trying to make conversation but you could sense they were not with you?

Have you ever spent hours looking for keys, glasses or documents, wasted hours of your time and energy, and lost your temper over it?

Have you ever missed the motorway exit because you were lost in your own thoughts?

Have you ever spent a whole day gathering dark thoughts despite having everything to smile about: a sunny day, your kids, a neighbour, a nice friend, and yet you didn't notice any of it?

Have you ever lost friends because you had tired them out with your constant worrying about everything?

Have you ever had that feeling of just not being connected?

All of this would no longer happen, or a lot less at least and a lot less intensely if you allowed yourself to live in the present moment.

You would waste less time and energy, you'd have fewer fears and regrets, you would allow more time for yourself and for others while being more authentic and objective, you would be less likely to dramatise things in your head (unless you wanted to), you'd have a greater capacity for making choices and taking on responsibilities in full awareness – the road to freedom – be better at making the most of the good times in life and to experience them fully and increase your capacity to keep things in perspective.

The list is long and I am stopping here. Take a good look at yourself and you'll get what I mean!

Doesn't living in the present all the time become rather tiresome?

On the contrary, but in any case you can rest assured – nobody does!

It is certainly less tiresome than stressing over the fact we can't remember where we've put our stuff, stressing over the fact that we're stressing for one thing or another, or because we've reacted in a way we later come to regret. We waste less time and energy when we are present. It may be obvious but it's not always easy. We often have to press the 'I am in the here and now' switch. And when we get round to it for just a few minutes, a few hours, what calm we experience!

They say sophrology helps develop creativity. How come?

In fact, what does being creative mean?

From where I stand and from my own experience of things, I would say that being creative means acting in the way that's right for our self at any given time. We are not just talking here about artistic creativity.

If you are sat in an armchair and after 10 minutes your back starts to ache, you can either choose to remain seated in that armchair and put up with it, or change your position, or change seat, get up and stand -that's included in the 'change position' bit above -, or place a cushion or two to support your back... If all you do when you are changing position is to change the way you place your legs or your bottom, at least you are the one making that decision.

Before you decide to modify your posture, you first have to be aware of the fact that it is possible for you to change and to do things differently.

Once you give yourself the possibility of doing things differently to improve your wellbeing, you are taking positive action to meet your needs. When you change your posture consciously because you notice the position you're in isn't comfortable, you are being creative. And in this sense, creativity is living.

In fact, to start off with, what you experience is fairly average: neither good nor bad. Then you become aware of what you're experiencing in the moment, your sensations, thoughts, emotions, feelings... and if what you notice isn't very pleasant, you can choose to stay with it or you can examine all the different possibilities that are offered to you and change accordingly. If we return to our earlier example with reference to modifying our posture; you can choose to walk, go and fetch a cushion, ask someone to get you a cushion or a footstool, relax, moan, complain or get tense... Now you know, all you do is make the right choice, (choices even), put it into action and take full responsibility for the choice that you made.

We always have a choice. At times, that choice may be very limited while at other times, most of the time in fact, there exists a wide range of possibilities on offer but we are not even aware of them. It's all about the way we look at things: the way we look at events, ourselves, our beliefs and our ideas, the way we live and the way we think.

Awareness in all its different forms is what we develop through the practice of sophrology. We develop a field of awareness of possibilities, especially the simplest ones, those we don't normally think about precisely because they are too simple!

When we develop our awareness of the possibilities available to us and the different ways we can look at our experiences, the way we are and think, our capacity for allowing ourselves to make a choice and to put that choice into action, to make changes, then the clear answer to the above question is yes! practising sophrology does develop our creativity.

You probably know people who say they can't change, and that's the way it is, and that nothing can be done about it, that they have no choice, right?

Well, it's up to us to turn our life into a creation of our own!

By means of a conclusion

There are certainly many other topics to talk about, but here is where I choose to stop. However, if you have any more questions you'd like answered, don't hesitate to let me know and I'll answer them if I can.

In my explanations, I used a lot of examples linked to the body since these were the most obvious ones for me to use as a sophrologist and teacher of physical education. I mostly referred to Caycedian dynamic relaxations since this is what I teach.

Other books are available on different subjects to complement my thoughts but I have no wish to duplicate these.

My book doesn't give definitions, doesn't tell the history nor does it describe sophrology techniques.

All I set out to do in answering these beginners' questions was to help them to persevere with sophrology. Some of the answers here can perhaps, in part, also relate to meditation, whatever its form.

If you have any questions on the biochemical functioning of the brain during and after a session, or on the different levels and states of consciousness, or on Caycedo and how sophrology came about, or on completely different matters such as how to learn to say no, how to manage conflicts, stop smoking or other personal development issues, you'll find plenty of other reference books in your local bookshop.

I hope I've filled the gap which up to now hadn't been filled. All I hope is that I've met my objective and that you feel you now know a little more about sophrology.

Finally, as a Tourette syndrome sufferer since age seven, I am now in the position some twenty years on, to honestly claim it is the discovery of sophrology that has saved me.

It has been for me the one and only approach... and the pillar of all my activities.

Thank you

My thanks go to my sophrology students and friends who encouraged me to write this book, telling me it would be a good idea to do it, that there was a need for it, and a gap there for me to fill!

Thanks to all those who, once my project came to their attention, welcomed my project with kindness, and without any conflict of ego.

My special thanks go to Soizick Roulinat, who in full knowledge of the facts, genuinely encouraged me to turn my project into a reality. I am grateful for his support and his exceptional attention.

Thanks to my two big boys who never laughed at their mother and took part in the page setting, especially Antoine the oldest, who did a really professional job of it!

Thanks to my husband who showed belief in me by taking me on a winter sports holiday! Since I don't ski, that is where I wrote three quarters of my book, while my three men were sliding down the slopes.

And to all of those who've understood that sophrology activates our capacity for questioning ourselves, and if they think it is tiresome, I tell them that from my own perspective and experience, it is a lot less tiresome to make progress than not to!

Finally, I am grateful to myself for the fact that in spite of my disability, I have completed this long-awaited project, and I congratulate myself for having done it.

And while on the subject, I thank you Bernard Santerre and all my teachers past and present from the bottom of my heart, for having accepted me as I am, despite the unease caused at times by my presence in class. Thank you for your absence of judgement and for your welcome. Your attitude and your teaching have taught me how to accept myself as I am.

Thanks to sophrology and to its great inventor!

Already published at BoD, in French:

*En quoi le fait de remuer les épaules
va m'aider à aller mieux dans ma vie ?*
(September 2014)

Haute en tics (December 2017)